Histo... MARVELLOUS Mistakes

Ciaran Murtagh

OXFORD
UNIVERSITY PRESS

Great Clarendon Street, Oxford, OX2 6DP, United Kingdom

Oxford University Press is a department of the University of Oxford. It furthers the University's objective of excellence in research, scholarship, and education by publishing worldwide. Oxford is a registered trade mark of Oxford University Press in the UK and in certain other countries

British Library Cataloguing in Publication Data
Data available

ISBN: 978-0-19-830806-5

10 9 8 7 6 5 4

Paper used in the production of this book is a natural, recyclable product made from wood grown in sustainable forests. The manufacturing process conforms to the environmental regulations of the country of origin.

Printed in China by Golden Cup

Acknowledgements

Series Editor: Nikki Gamble
Cover illustration: David Semple

Illustrations by David Semple

The publishers would like to thank the following for the permission to reproduce photographs: **p11:** Charles J Sharp/Wiki Commons; **p12t:** Bettman/Corbis; **p12b:** Photo Researchers/Mary Evans Picture Library; **p17:** Mary Evans Picture Library/Alamy; **p18:** Bettman/Corbis; **p18-23** (background): CNRI/Science Photo Library; **p20:** Food & Drug Administration/Science Photo Library; **p23:** Steve Vidler/Alamy.

Contents

Marvellous Mistakes

Everybody makes mistakes! I do. Once I made my dad sneeze off his moustache!

But mistakes aren't always bad. Some brilliant things were only discovered by mistake.

Let's meet the people behind three of history's most marvellous mistakes!

The explorer **Christopher Columbus** found a new **continent**, which he wasn't even looking for!

Who put that there?

The healthy **Kellogg brothers** invented breakfast cereal by accident!

Shh! I'm working!

And **Dr Alexander Fleming** invented a new medicine by going on holiday!

Christopher Columbus

Christopher Columbus, 1451–1506

Christopher Columbus was born in 1451. People think he first went to sea when he was ten. Before that, people say he helped his father sell cheese.

Bye, Dad!

CHEESE

At sea, Columbus learned different languages. He learned about **tides** and how to find his way using the stars. By 1492, he was ready to make his marvellous mistake!

In Columbus's time, people could sail from Europe to Asia, but the **route** was dangerous.

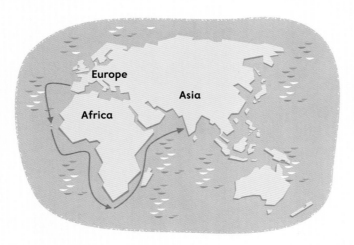

Columbus thought he could find a quicker and safer route by heading west. In 1492, he set sail to prove it. No one knew there was a continent in the way.

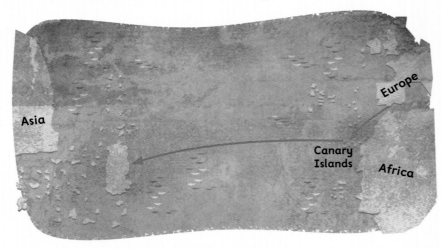

Columbus's planned route

The journey took ten weeks.

Columbus thought he had arrived in Asia. But actually, he had found the continent of America!

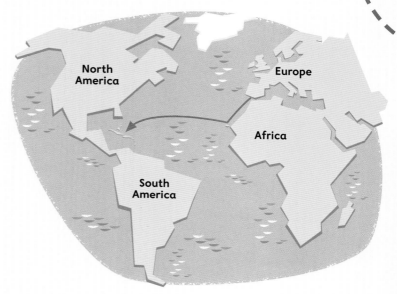

Columbus's actual route

9

Columbus stayed and explored.

Then he went back
and told everyone
about what he
called 'Western Asia'.
The discovery made
him rich.

Columbus died in 1506, still convinced that the land he had found was part of Asia.

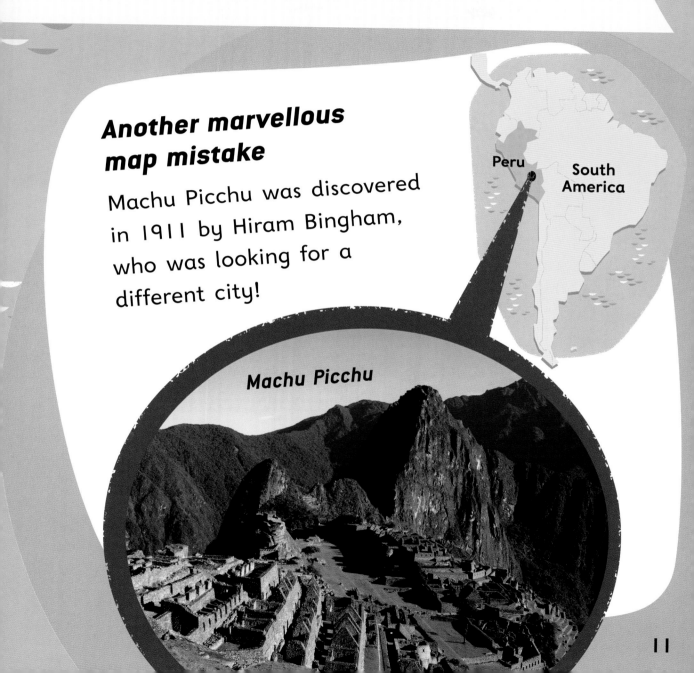

Another marvellous map mistake

Machu Picchu was discovered in 1911 by Hiram Bingham, who was looking for a different city!

Peru

South America

Machu Picchu

The Kellogg Brothers

Will Kellogg, 1860–1951

John and **Will Kellogg** were two American brothers, born in the mid-1800s.

John was a doctor. He and Will ran a **health resort** where they taught other people about healthy food and exercise.

John Kellogg, 1852–1943

In the 1890s, breakfast wasn't always a very healthy meal.

John and Will decided to invent a new, healthier breakfast. On 8th August 1894, they made their marvellous mistake.

The brothers were cooking wheat to make healthy bread. Then they were called away.

When they came back, the wheat had gone **stale**.

14

They made flakes out of the stale wheat.

John and Will toasted the flakes. They tasted good! The brothers tried out different **grains** and found that flakes made with corn tasted best.

Serious cereal statistic

The world's largest bowl of cereal held 1000 kilograms of cornflakes.

In 1906, the brothers argued. Will wanted to add sugar to the recipe. John did not.

Will set up his own cornflake factory and called it Kellogg's.

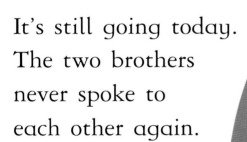

It's still going today. The two brothers never spoke to each other again.

Another marvellous munchable mistake

Chocolate chip cookies were invented in 1911 by Ruth Graves Wakefield while she was trying to make chocolate-flavoured cookies.

Alexander Fleming

Alexander Fleming, 1881–1955

Alexander Fleming

was born in Scotland in 1881. He was a doctor who studied bacteria. Bacteria are tiny bugs that are too small to be seen. Some bacteria can cause diseases.

In the First World War, Fleming worked as a doctor. He noticed that many soldiers died because harmful bacteria **infected** their wounds.

He started looking for a cure.
This led to his marvellous mistake.

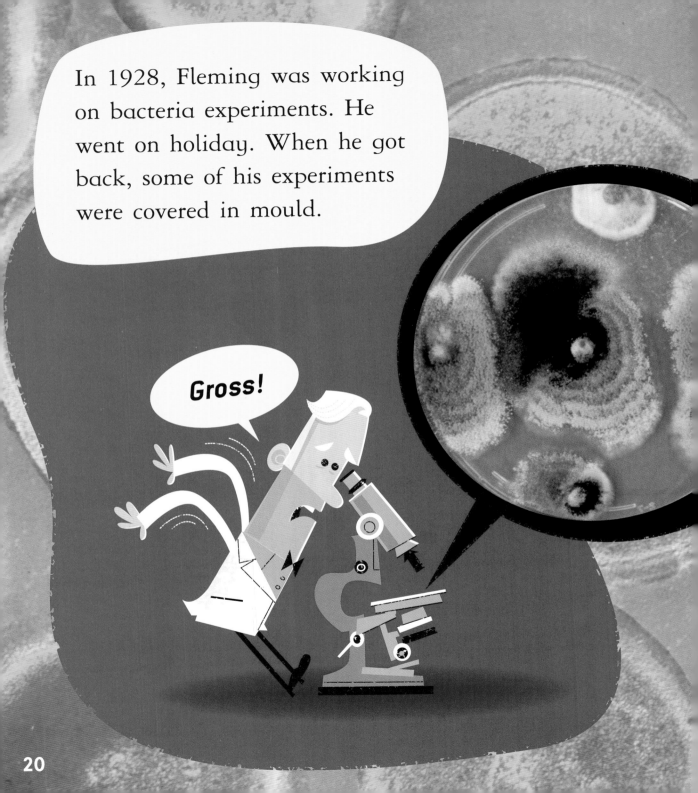

In 1928, Fleming was working on bacteria experiments. He went on holiday. When he got back, some of his experiments were covered in mould.

Some of the mould had killed the harmful bacteria. It was the cure Fleming had been looking for! He called his discovery 'mould juice' – but he soon changed the name to penicillin (*say* pen-i-sil-in).

Would you like some mould juice?

Fleming couldn't find a way to turn his discovery into medicine. But other scientists continued his work. In 1941, they started treating people with their new medicine – the first antibiotics (*say* an-tee-bigh-o-tiks).

Another marvellous medical mistake

X-rays were discovered in 1895 by Wilhelm Röntgen, who was studying something else.

Antibiotics have saved millions of lives. Fleming's **laboratory** is now a museum.

So don't worry if you get lost, burn your toast or forget to tidy your room! Your mistake might just change the world!

Glossary

continent: one of the world's main large areas of land

grains: cereal crops used as food, like wheat, rice, barley or corn

health resort: a place you can visit to learn to be more healthy

infected: filled with disease

laboratory: a room where you can do scientific experiments

route: the way to get from one place to another

stale: dry and no longer good to eat

tides: movements of the sea, caused by the moon

Index